*slight faith*

Praise for *slight faith*

"The beauty of faith isn't so much about paradise as it is
the absence before, the gap we must leap in order to land.
In her meditative and profound book *slight faith*, Risa
Denenberg plants her feet before the divide, wrestles with
the angels of loss and doubt. 'There is nothing,' Denenberg
writes, 'on the other side for certainty to dine on.' Yet,
there is so much in this book that nourishes.

'These are days of awe,' she writes and while reading
these poems I too am opened up to a sense of fear and
wonder. These poems speak to the sacred within and
outside of us. There is death and pain but inevitably there
is 'the slipperiness of hope.' There is an almost reluctant
acceptance of pleasure. 'I've grown passably / fond of
rain,' she says and I can't help but smile as she tries for
something 'more pastoral.'

Despite the scope of Denenberg's poetry, which spans
generations and religions and loves, her talent for restraint
offers the subtle power and influence of a musical score.
It is a difficult and fine balance to strike. Although she
may write from and for the perspective of those who only
praise or lament, she recognizes the very different silences
that come after. We are given invaluable moments of
introspection. Tightly crafted, wise with a quietly passionate
heart, *slight faith* will make a reader leap and marvel."
—Michael Schmeltzer, author of *Blood Song*

"*slight faith* is what we need in these extraordinary
times and Risa Denenberg offers us this and more in her
personal how-to manual for survival: 'train for comedy
and calamity,' she urges. From Babylon to New York
City, these luminous poems travel via polished lines and
prescient language. Yet, the voyage is never easy. The poet
keeps vigil alongside the dying and the dead but these
poems exist in service to the living. It's as if Denenberg
has split open her life and scraped out the interior fruit.

Judaism, Buddhism, yoga, and all night car rides—
the speaker scours each for answers. Across decades,
families, and the names of trees, we experience 'this
double helix called love.' This is a collection that I plan
to return to, to read again the music of 'sozzle,' 'trundle,'
and 'roil;' to revel in the alchemy of 'everyday clouds that
amaze.' As a Jewish woman poet, I am especially excited
to welcome this book into the world."
                    —Susan Rich, author of *Cloud Pharmacy*

"*slight faith* is not an easy read, but one infused with
intelligence, a questioning mind, a deep sadness that
offers to the reader a kind of solace, an invitation to join
hands with, together to appreciate the curves and stresses
of life. There are glimpses of peace too, a respite in the
meditative 'Fifty Breaths,' a prescription for tranquility
in 'How to Be Sad' ('May you hear the stillness between
breakers'). My favorite poem, perhaps, is 'Famous'—a
tour-de-force plummeting through a life, its long lines
reflecting its rant-like tone and sweep, its power grabbing
us, pulling us in. I admire the honesty and straight-
seeing-ness of Denenberg's journey, her courage to look
deeply into the 'ordeal of living,' to share boldly a world
in which, Job-like, we find a mirror of ourselves."
                    —Laura Foley, author of *Night Ringing*

# slight faith

### RISA
### DENENBERG

MoonPathPress

Poetry
ISBN 978-1-936657-35-3

Cover art: painting by Hilma af Klint,
titled *The Dove*, No. 5 (1915)

Author photo: Ronda Broatch

Design: Tonya Namura
using Minion Pro (text) and Guess Pro (display)

MoonPath Press is dedicated to publishing the finest poets
of the U.S. Pacific Northwest.

MoonPath Press
PO Box 445
Tillamook, OR 97141

MoonPathPress@gmail.com

http://MoonPathPress.com

*For Faith,*
*her unfaithful lover,*
*her agnostic wife,*
*and their daughter,*
*slight faith.*

*To Kindness*

*acts of kindness always*
*make me cry*
*don't know why*
*you might suspect*
*I haven't had my share*
*but surely no one is ever sated*
*with kindness*
*and each simple kindness*
*is a prayer for kindness*
*knelt in supplication for more*
*kindness to be offered*
*in spaces where*
*there is no kindness*
*to spare*

# Contents

# three

# four

slight faith

*one*

*Faith is a fine invention.*
*—Emily Dickinson*

# Before World

*Now the earth was formless and void,*
*and darkness was over the surface of the deep.*
*—Genesis 1:2*

Birds don't sing.
Jazz don't swing.
Bees don't hive.
Men don't jive.

Life swims before it flies.
Life crawls before it leaps.

Before houses, men don't build prisons.
Before fences, coyotes don't kill chickens.
And then earth is partitioned.

Trees teach birds to perch.
Birds teach frogs to jump.
Frogs teach girls to skip rope.
Girls teach words to sing.

Songs sing before sin.
Sins teach women to pray.
And then prayers teach hate.

Before prayer,
Women aren't spoils of war.
Black men don't swing from trees.
Landmines don't amputate boys.
Kids don't drown in the sea.

## Metanoia Lost

I speak god language
because people die
and god is the tongue of death.

Death stopped time, left me behind
my father with the small pot of raspberry jam
he ate with a spoon.

My story-line is a birth, a chipped
tooth, an affair, a custody war, a death by fire,
a vial of ash.

It's no different than yours—
a flash-memory in the shower,
a bruise without details.

Life offers tautologies—
*there is no god but god.*
Can words offer a morsel of faith?

There was no conversion the day
I fell from grace
and lost my name on the road.

Lost is an actual place, you know.

## Saving Moses

There were rushes and a stream, a swathed infant
in a basket floating, and no Miriam in sight.
I wanted to save Moses from the dry scorch
of the desert, the crash of tablets, his futile
vexation with idol worshipers, but he was bade
to slay the overseer and split the sea. I had to
nurse him and let him go.

All the water on this planet—the ponds and rivulets,
the swells and torrents, the sinkhole in Miami
where we took turns swinging from a rope
into the bottomless azure—these waters
run their courses, but will not save us.

## The Slightness of Faith

Having stumbled on faith,
I've learned how little it mollifies, how slapdash the veil
that seemed bountiful as the sky, how narrow the channel
once entered.

A moment submerged in faith,
and my attention scuttles back to its foxhole to shroud
what I've allowed too close. I've watched how hands at prayer
plead for tenure on earth.

Having stumbled on faith,
I've learned to speak in tongues. I've learned to bless and
curse. I've opened up my purse and slept in dens of whores.
I've cried and not known why.

Faith knows there is nothing
on the other side for certainty to dine on, no ode of ovation
or aroma of baking bread, no fond family reunions, only
the fission of all the familiar.

Faith will always be for sale,
and men of cloth have always lied. No angel watches over
me, although I pray for one. *My God,* I lost my only son.
Is my god done with me?

## Quarter-Mile Church

Because faith is a hand with a missing thumb,
she can't hitch a ride to church. She dwells
under the house with the possums and feral cats.
She eats refuse. Invited indoors, she'll refuse
to take a seat or drink tea. Her dress will be dowdy
or she'll show up naked and ravenous. She'll claim
coin you don't have. Sooner or later, you'll glimpse her
running reckless on a winding country road
where lordly pines hem the curves like needlepoint.
You'll sense her slight genuflection, hazy and just
out of view, shushing your cries while retrieving
the knife from your hand with her missing thumb.

And for an instant you'll be unafraid.
It will last no more than quarter-mile.

## Southern Faith

comes to the door
wagging a tale for sweet iced tea, then sways
her hips, serene on the porch swing, sipping
between handfuls of boiled peanuts.

I didn't invite her here, you know.
But I'm always the obliging one
mimicking Southern slang,
*If you don't feed her, she's a goner.*

I left the South in a flurry
of blunders. Yet here she is
in Seattle, whistling gospel
for anyone with ears.

## Charoset and Bitter Herbs

An amalgam of ground walnuts, chopped apples,
red wine and nutmeg
primes us to recall the taste of mortar—

the timeworn saga of servitude and how despots'
sovereignties always hinge on slavery.
But instead, it is sweet as honey

and reminds us that all history is gloss,
and how repetition, like nostalgia,
adds narcotic notes of harmony to bitter herbs.

You were mortar, when I needed horseradish
to loosen tears. You float into view
and I cringe at what I did to push you away.

Sweet and bitter are bound and every year
I recant vows with sips of soured wine.
It is only myself I risk enslaving,

immersed as I am in this freedom song.
As penance, I sometimes wonder
what it was I did to deserve you.

# Formation

*You knit me together in my mother's womb.*
*—Psalm 139*

During formation, the nuns enlighten the novices,
the novices instruct the postulants, and the postulants
direct the aspirants, *don't form particular friendships,*
meaning, *shun sexual feelings.*

Mums mold their own children, while scrubbing
pots and peeling potatoes. They say, *stay.*
They say, *stick to your own,* they imply,
*this primal love affair could last forever.*

Buddhist monks say little, impart impossibilities.
*Form no attachments, eat no animals, forgive*
*the slayers of your family and your nation.* They sit
zazen and don't expound.

I'm not sure what love is, or how.
No palpable lust snags at my heart. I notice
how *these* pine slats and legs form *this* chair. Any
old chair may cast shadows on the floor, whorls

and splinters dangling like stalactites that might last
eons or melt tomorrow. Form is my foremost quandary,
after love. It's always changing. And I'm always
searching for something that's gone missing.

Not that I've never wanted a starry-eyed lover.
But can arms hold ephemera? If all the gods,
a convent of nuns, an abiding mother, a bushel
of monks, a muse or such, would clutch me

bosom snug, unzip my flesh and admire the pith,
well, that would surely be something. Admitting
that I don't know what love is, is also something,
perhaps a better thing. Or the only thing,

since it is mine. I can't love each creamy bud
on the dogwood tree in the yard, every fat-bellied
ant running the countertop in the kitchen. And
no matter how hard I try, *so sorry*, but I can't love you.

## Consolation

Imagine the crawl from sight to sightlessness.
Even in dreams you wear bifocals.

Imagine not knowing your grandson's name, or being
lost in a word-salad thicket of sinister trees.

Imagine lying on your death bed, palms cupped
in a mudra of surrender. And among dementia,

going blind, and dying, you pray death will come first.
This is how you curl into your solace, bidding its shell

to your mollusk, storm of sea blowing in your ear,
inexpressible pain expressed *sotto voce*.

## Abiding Winter

How we made it through another winter's
not the question. Nor is it an answer
since one of us was left behind in winter.

In Spring, in buoyancy, you asked a question.
Cups stood their ground between us, tea and coffee.
You wished to be the answer to your question.

Then winter comes again and yet another,
a darkling season full of melancholy. The yanking
of my soul back to the gutter, that other

place where questions have no answers,
and answers only placate. It takes rafters
of steadfast faith, or mettle, to seek answers.

Truth is brutal. So much we can't recover,
years I've begged for you to wait for Spring to bloom
again, living in despair beside each other, and another

stormy season while we tussle for an answer
or a coda to the sum of all of life's bother.
I've learned to hold my tongue, to question
nothing. Questions are another sort of winter.

*two*

*Its place remembers it no more.*
*—Psalm 103*

## Exiled in Babylon

*How can we sing the Lord's song in a foreign land?*
*—Psalm 137*

We sit and weep by the rivers of Babylon.
Where we are forced to sing for our captors.
Where we are exiled without a place to call home.

We beg our God to smash their children's heads against
    rocks.
Because we loathe war, but even more despise captivity.
Because we are afraid we might marry the wrong person.

We hang our lyres on poplars and refuse to sing wedding
    songs.
But then we agree, under some duress, to marry someone
    we barely know.
And then our betrotheds betray us, sleeping with younger
    women.

We drive all night across an endless sea of land to California.
For our dwellings, with their thin white walls, make living
    a grey affair.
For our children renounce us, forever to wander in diaspora.

The children of Babylon shall have no roots, not even in
    Los Angeles.
Truly we shall be expats to the umpteenth generation.
Truly we've tried to gain purchase in every nation to no avail.

We didn't know the housing code would make us pay for
    our own repairs.
Meanwhile it rains all night and the roof leaks.
Meanwhile the bowl overflows in the carpeted bathroom,
    and it's disgusting.

19

Our lives are shattered and our history is rejected with
form letters.
Regrettably, we've not prepared for our future, which is
extinction.
Regretfully, we'll sit and weep forever, in this valley of
idols.

# In Search of Home

From Rittenhouse to First Avenue, Tallahassee to Sequim,
I've grown tomatoes on fire escapes, sketched maps
on kitchen cabinets, pinned post cards onto walls,
only to leave hundreds of tiny holes when I depart.

I always depart. Things don't work out as planned.
I clash with the boss and get fired. My lover
takes a lover. I feel hemmed in and need to escape
the hundreds of tiny holes in my heart.

The hole in my heart makes its absence known.
The doctors are not hopeful. I refuse to moan
as long as there is time to wail sad ballads, to mourn
lost mornings and my hundreds of tiny blunders.

The huge and tiny blunders, kitchen to kitchenette,
bed to couch. If I don't fade away right now,
I'll join the old folks who sit at card-tables holding
paper cups, swallowing hundreds of tiny sips.

Life is a bowl of tiny sips from which I have
swilled my share. What seems to loom large is,
after all, only one short life, this teeny-tiny stint
of time to partake, to embrace, to quietly depart.

## Swimming Lesson
*—for Buddy*

Florida panhandle, that eddy
    within a stream of tannin-washed
backwaters, bitter and ferrous, lined with glabrous white
    quartz, limestone and moonstone. And deep quarries,
rope-entry only, water so clear and cold you could
    see your toes shrivel. Effortless bike rides on aimless
sweaty summer days, cheap wine packed in a ripped brown
    canvas rucksack.

Lost Lake is still on the map, but it's not the same lake
    I crossed, leaving old Sassafras on muddy sand,
unbound and water-shy. And that day I swam with sure
    breaststrokes, you hidden in the pine-wrapped shore
watching my body do its work, steady and pliant,

and later, when we stopped at a barn junkyard
    you bought a ceramic bowl, glazed with tiny red and
purple blossoms, a slightly chipped bargain, still bearing
    fruit in my Seattle kitchen, miles, years, time-zones
(and something intangible, mislaid, prized for its absence)
    away.

# Mean Distance from the Sun, Mid-Winter, Northern Hemisphere

I lie fallow in my seventh decade
91 million miles
from an imploding fireball
beheld as light
that raced eight minutes
to reach my eyes
and has mercifully allowed me
the miracle
of another breakfast.

*(Two shiny eggs*
*smothered in salsa*
*atop a tortilla; pined for*
*in preparation; fleeting*
*as an orgasm.)*

I sit at a table
27 hundred miles
from the southern tip of the Florida coast
a knife, a fork
grasped firmly in two hands
and cut myself
into pieces small enough
for a child to swallow.

Nothing is simple.
Not our distance from the sun
nor my distance from my son.

## Ice Would Suffice

How swift, how far
the sea
carries a body from shore.

Empires fail, species are lost,
spotted frogs
and tufted puffins forsaken.

After eons of fauna and flora, hominids have stood
for mere years
baffled brains atop battered shoulders.

In a murky blanket of heavens
an icy planet
made of diamond spins.

Our sun winks like the star
it was
billions of years ago, without ambition.

We bury bodies in shallow dirt, heedless of lacking space
or how long
our makeshift planet will host us.

# How Two Trees Become a Forest
*—for Arthur Sze*

A teacher draws Chinese characters on the chalkboard
to show how two trees become a forest. Chalk is soft
white limestone composed of the shells of foraminifers.
A student looks up the Chinese character for shell. An
Afghani schoolgirl covers her head and walks to the
schoolhouse with broken windows. She tells her teacher
she hopes to become a doctor. I bring soup to a neighbor
who tells me she hopes to die soon. The girl on the radio
sings, *my body's in trouble.* I wonder will I die alone.
A lonely boy pauses in front of a girl sketching a forest
of firs and yews. Their branches barely move in the humid
haze of noon. An infant grabs the wooden slats of her crib
and pulls herself up to cry out for her mother. I think how
much is lost without these signs to guide us. Foraminifers
are single-celled amoebae. The foramen ovale is a hole
in the heart that must close at birth.

# Life Forms Evolving

I think too much.
It doesn't help.

Turn off the news,
it spreads belly up
like every dead thing

molting, putrefying
conclave of the next
offspring without feathers.

Ebola didn't mean
to be so fierce,
dying in its own

stewpot of blood
and vomit. It needs
to tone down

the rhetoric
and it will
(scientists predict)

become less fatal,
more contagious—
a bee sting

like Hep C or
Kekulé's benzene ring
busily mutating HIV.

Nothing sentient
or stone knows
why it's here,

or what will
become of it.
Disturbing, yes.

But don't make too much
of bones or whales,
of pathogens or wings.

Later, they'll become
other things.

## Bimbo, a Deer Story

For she had no body odor and lay motionless
beside the dead doe, and so
you took her home and fed her goat's milk.

This you did: collared and tethered her, named her
Bimbo, a pet wandering a yard strewn with cars
on blocks and old oil tanks.

Your darling: adopted, broken, stroked, chosen.
And who am I, trussed and bound to a fault line,
who shadowed not her own mother, nor knows
how she is meant to be.

# Outsider

I live in a small town of recovered alcoholics
who go to weeknight meetings to drink coffee
and gossip. These good people also go to church
on Sundays to hear sermons drawn from within
the town's close-cropped borders and offer prayers
to heal sins they will later talk about over Reuben
paninis at the Longhouse.

I'm the oddball: vegetarian lesbian poet
who celebrates Pesach to their Easter, rents instead
of owns, has never married, chooses to live alone.

Last week I bought a push mower and huffed
around my yard snipping the tall grass and elfin
pink and violet flowers down to nubbins. I did
this to ward off chatter among my friendly neighbors
over my overgrown habits, although I know they think
it's strange to not eat meat and refuse to waste
gas on this endeavor. If I wait too long, someone
will come along and mow down my whole house
out of kindness.

As for me, I love the tall grasses, the bees sniffing
a sprinkling of petals. I welcome deer to come
graze in my yard, lush with dandelions.

# Terminal

The jet that is coming to whoosh me away
has not yet arrived at the terminal, which is where I am
always, and when it touches tarmac, when it taxis to the
gate, there will be other delays—hail and brimstone,
a sozzled pilot, a cat in the cockpit. I'm not in charge
of the weather but I've packed ample provisions.

Still, I follow its whereabouts relentlessly, it's so easy
to do, what with google maps and the crisscross
of satellites telling us where we are and how many
steps we take each day. I sometimes go offline to unwind.
I reckon it's unassailably on its way, delays are just that,
I don't want to appear too eager. I do hover close
so as not to miss the announcements. An ailing passenger
might swap places with me in line.

All I want is to chill with my book and munch
my lunch. Before long, I'll organize what's left
into rubbish, compost, and recollections. There'll be
a damp spot on the bench when I rise. I'll wave
fond farewells and board when my row is called.

# three

Who is my mother? And who are my brethren?
—Matthew 12:48

## Camels and Iced Coffee

I was relieved she fell the spring before the towers fell,
after making her way through Spanish Flu, World War II,
the loss of her first child, who would have been,

*was*, my sister. In the constellation of family,
her unformed body is a still black hole in the night sky.
If I edge too close, my mother's downcast glance finds me.

I'd rather think casually of her Camels and iced coffee,
the cirrus clouds of smoke rising as swirls of milk tumble
through the chocolaty liquid, slow to wholly embrace.

As was she. Ashtrays crammed full of lipsticked butts
were nasty, the bitter drink was icy, nothing like
the honeyed voice and cushy bosom I craved. But as I begin

to look and sound so much like her, I see how loss
has desiccated me too. I now regard her leftover love
without ire or irony, forgiving almost everything.

# Driving Lesson

My father taught me how to drive
How to take curves without braking
First, slow down
Then, push deep into it
Letting speed itself
Moor you to the road
Like moon rounding earth

I think of him
As I traverse life's breaks and turns
And the days he took me driving
Letting go slowly, deeply
His faith in centripetal force
The laws of physics that held us together
As we spun out of control

## In which my brother goes to
## her grave and I shed a tear

My brother goes to the grave
site and says farewell
to the engraving on the rock.

I live far away and today
the buttress crumbles and I miss my mother
for the first time.

I don't know why he does it
knowing and not knowing him so well
is all I have to go on.

Debt, veneration, relief, it's all
so mixed, right? Maybe in his melancholy
he hoards an image of our family,

but I feel misplaced today, weepy
as if disowned, shorn from that photo
not like me at all, the cold unfeeling

bitch of me, knowing and not knowing
myself so well, with no urge to go on
after so many years.

# Map of Death by Drowning

my mother slashed the rugs
then patched them back together mishmash around the
house
my father bit the apple
and tore the map of death in two
together they drove me to the river
I tried to protest, but couldn't clear my throat for all the
corn in Iowa
something jammed, a trickle of chokecherry wine
chafing my windpipe
I couldn't shake the taste of regurgitated hawk
my heart bruited the news, a bravura broadcast
of my drowning, all the tattered bits of fabric were laid
end-to-end on my bloated belly and I clasped one-half of
the map
in my right hand, the other half left to rot while
I could utter nothing, not even

ahem

## Faith's Cavity

Faith is the slight stalk clutching
tight the baby tooth to its root.
If it won't let go, a father might
tie a string and slam the door.
A mother might calmly let it fall
among the bedclothes while the child
sleeps. Some find coin beneath
a pillow once it's gone. But what
promises another truth will descend
from this cavity to fill what's lost?

## Tracings

I gather my belongings and retrace my steps.
I left you once, not for good.
There was a child between us.
I trace my hands in a sketchbook and color them gray.
This is an ordinary sort of unbelonging.
On an ordinary day without any sort of hand-holding.
I'd rather not touch.
That was all a long time ago but is still between us.
I trace my hand in a sketchbook and color it bruised.
I've discovered that tracings are warrens of lost content.
The child in my arms was pulled away.
His small arms reached for mine.
That was all a long time ago, but still.
If you read our biography. (There is no biography.)
If you go looking for me. (You will not go looking.)
I have gathered my belongings and retraced my steps so
      many times.
I'm not going to list my losses. Use your imagination.

## Nostalgia is an illness you might die of

Last winter I lit a candle, placed it in the window
to guide the night birds to me so I could sleep.
Morning now. I face a slice of pink sky and await
words, dormant bulbs interred in dirt. Your absence
invades my slumber, I will die of it. The rawness
is too much. The final verdict was disclosed
as the blinds were closing, closed. I think of when
we sat at the rough-hewn table where we speared
pears and dared lay slices in each other's mouths
with the knife. Maybe you believe in angels still.

I should ask for help—
a kiss, a pill.

# The Better Part
### —*Luke 10:38-42*

In the village, two sisters shared a household.
Martha the elder cooked, chopped wood,
did laundry, made beds. Mary was lazy.

Martha fed strangers, Mary was a chatterbox.
Martha's pleas for relief, even shaming,
meant nothing to Mary. So, who had the better part?

The food was good, the beds were soft, but the stranger
chose Mary, quick and poised, and whisked her away,
never to return. "Martha, Martha," the stranger rebuked

at the door, "you worry and fret about so many
things, yet few are needed." She replied, "You lie.
Food is Blood, Cleanliness is Body."

Martha got a cat, kept her larder full. Never
turned away drifters, but turned Mary's picture
to the wall. Wouldn't answer if she called.

We are hurt most by those who claim to love us.
A venomous hug, a misplaced kiss. The one who tore
us into pieces, choosing only our most delectable parts.

Mother held back praise, father drooled affection.
Teacher put us in a pen and forgot to water and feed.
Then the years of trying to patch the fragments,

to display our hidden portions, while crouching
behind the masturbator's seat, listening to lies
about our faces, our breasts, our tiny feet.

## How to Be Sad

If you listen without language, you may hear
my grandfather playing Brahms on the cello,
grunting every now and then with the effort
of an old man soon to die. He played for me

that spring I lay sick with pneumonia.
I was nine and lonely for my mothership,
her planets and galaxies preparing me
for a life of stargazing and solitude.

Although at times I say too much, there is much
I will never say. If you are sad, go to the ocean.
There, is music. Lay your tongue aside, listen.
May you hear the stillness between breakers.

# To a woman I might have loved
*—for Nancy*

I raised my hand to my forehead, scanning—
(*I don't know what for, was it fever or despair?*)

hearing my father had died, unable
to reach his body before its burial

I brought my hand to my breast, thinking
heartburn or infarction and wept for him,

for others, for all my corpses

but that was years ago, and then I hear
that yesterday you raised your hand

to your forehead and buckled, rushed
by helicopter to Harborview never knowing

(*was it stroke or lost hope?*)

a scribbled message that fell into my lap
from a woman I've never met (*your friend*)

said, *taken off life support*, but the image—
the hand, the puzzled brow, the collapse

so vivid

and how did she know to call me, you and I
(*can I say we?*) had only just met, and did she know

you had written a poem, sent it to me, as if
seeking my advice about poetry, until

(*another hand-to-head moment*) I realized it was
you, flirting, but instead of dinner or shy embrace

you are dead. Last night I dreamed our first
kiss, our last kiss, as you darkly departed.

*four*

*They call me and I go.*
—*William Carlos Williams*

## Yellow Star

In my case, the yellow star
will be made of two perfect pink triangles
cut from cheap dry goods
at the Triangle Shirtwaist Factory
where the women
sew stars on at the ready
hunched over their Singers
and, not wasting time on stairs,
work right up to closing time, then jump.

They didn't want to die so young
and neither did the gay boys who died in droves
at the close of the last century. I would be one
who would beg you to shoot me
who would know that borders lie
that I could not endure the march through the woods
in the snow to the trains at the end.

We who say never forget
also know that it could happen again
to us
and we do not know more now
than we did then
how to make it stop.

The stitching never ends. For practice,
I have sutured my arm to my sleeve
with triangles made from pages torn
from the Book of Job.

# Diaspora

*—For Aylan, Galip and Rehan Kurdi*

I see them in nightmares, or when muted in meditation.
There, they were doctors, green-grocers, stone masons.
Here, they snake around barricades like a river.

I see them when I'm working in clinic
listening to lungs or dressing a wound,
staying late to finish notes, weary and irritable.

I see them when I inch in traffic or hike a mountain trail.
There, they ate breakfast, went to jobs, read the daily,
made love. Here, they lie dead on highways like roadkill.

I see them in the church on Christmas day
where I serve ham and mashed potatoes because
after all, I'm Jewish and have nowhere else to be.

I see them in the shower and when I pray
(which I do sporadically) and I envisage them
streaming as a long bridge across sinister waters

full of vipers, swelling the roads to a town near you.
There, they were proud of their kids' report cards.
Here they struggle to keep children from drowning.

I pray to see them and to not see them
because it's so much worse than I can fathom
and I can't imagine an act that could make it right.

I see them as my family, ghettoed in their Russian shtetel,
then crossing the ravenous Atlantic to an unknown fate.
There, they prayed and were slaughtered.
Here, we forget to pray, and prosper.

# Mourning after Murders
*—For the murdered at Pulse, Orlando 6/12/2016*

I knew I was changed
when memories began pouring
over the disquiet and despair
tempering and cleansing me
into a dwindling bar of soap, shapeless as tallow
dissolved in a split stream reflection
reminding me that I was,

No, I *am*, queer
and, to my utter consternation,
(lost as I had been in hibernation)
still in need of some sort
of caress, some clemency
from privation, a sudden urge
for intimacy, for nuptials,
for the bonds of kinship—
to offset the horror.

The calloused pressure points on my soles
that once evoked tears were roiling again,
letting free sobs that embraced both loss
and longing. *Don't leave me. Please,
don't leave me like this.*

I even dreamt that my mother birthed
again, gave me a little sister to cherish,
and flayed my flesh, now unfastened,
to sprout this repatriation.

## "Body of well-known naturalist found in river" *

A woman wanders to escape. Her noetic life has dwindled
        down to grandchildren she never sees and a failure
to remember their names. She retains an ossified memory
        of the taxonomy of birds, but has lost her car keys
for the last time. She missmates the buttons on her flannel
        jacket. There is no one to straighten it or care,
no one to straighten her affairs—

not the trysts of mid-life, but the sort that bury you under
        piles of junk in your seventies. Physically, she is strong
with steady heart and unburnt lungs; she can hike for hours
        wielding a hand-carved walking stick, backpack
not a burden, canvas for shade or to lie upon, enough water
        for a day. She roams the path along the river where
she knows the flora and the pitch of bird calls.

The weekly chat with her daughter came this morning
        at ten. She no longer looks forward to these calls,
but does her best to fake it. Pleasantries were tendered
        and repaid. No hint was given of any plan or prayer.
In the river, tiny eyelets open within eddies as she slides
        from bank to current with a splash.
She is a perfect pear-shaped sea-bound droplet.

* found headline

## Of Countless Deaths

Of countless deaths today,
I witnessed two. To witness
any death is to feel desperately
alive. To discern that one's own

body lingers at the border between
here and not here. To experience
the shockwave of foreboding. To slip
into a moment of groundless grace.

And if you ask, as some do, why
I chose this vocation, this sitting
at the bedsides of the dying, I will
say, *because I can*. What else sustains

the private love I have for witness
is mystery, even to myself.

## "Even the Gorgeous Royal Chariots Wear Out" *

A single woman plans her own death.
She means to die before her body
betrays her further. Before her sickness
consumes the kindness of caregivers.

She imagines farewells, beloved
friends gathered at bedside.
But she needs to be alone. She craves
one more good night's sleep.

She composes her own elegy, intones
Buddhist chants. She hears a cappella,
Aeolian harps, hands slapping thighs.
She needs silence.

She is troubled, exhausted, can't go on
suffering like this. Still, she yearns to live.

She tries to swallow this cup while begging
you to take it from her, flush it down
the toilet, tell her there's been a reprieve.

Friends come and go, wave incense,
chant and pray, try to shape a seamless
channel. She sends them away. *Come
back tomorrow*, she says.

And now the entourage is leaving, one by one,
to dogs and kids and partners. None can spend
another night at this vigil.

So it is her, alone, as she thought it would be.
As it should be. When her moment.
Comes to pass.

*from a Buddhist deathbed chant

# Two Women Gaze into the Same Abyss

One in danger,
fleeing a world of torment: mindsick,
homeless, breadless

while I lean over the other's bed
in a room with shelves full of teddy bears
and gently coax medicine

down her throat, the empty bottle
labeled with her name and the words:
*fatal if swallowed.*

The first one I can't help. Her e-mails
are puzzling. I don't know what realm she aches for
or where she will sleep tonight.

The other has chosen her own plot.
Tonight, at least, dying
seems easier than running.

# Twenty Years of Dead
### —*for Jon (1956-1993)*

There's not a lot of love that isn't brutal, but we

had our East Village dives that didn't open for Sunday
liquid-brunch until 1 pm and Monday nights at the G&L
Community Center where all the boys were cruising and
you hung out with me anyway, and

your pâté, your miraculous leg of lamb, your
hundred layers of filo, and

your ten plagues, the infusions that didn't kill
the germ that killed you, and how

after I met your parents, and
after I found the shoebox of postcards of martyred Saints
and slush pile of short stories you wrote in college,
I read your journals.

*I should never have read your journals.*

Your love was hilarious
and full of grand gestures and
caution tossed, and

Christ how we could talk smart and fast like 2 Jews do,
I could meet up with you after an AA meeting, count
on you to say *good god girl, you need a drink*, because

you knew you were going to die and you could say
things so brainsick as *after I die, I want you to burn
my body in the street and eat my flesh.*

## The Night We Tossed Your Ashes

mingled with rose petals
into the whitecaps at Cherry Grove

*can you see us*

standing at the eastern edge
of sand at midnight
and the others, your friends
stampeding into waves
at high tide butt-naked
calling to me

*come in come in come in*

because of you
I have ebbed
into a bystander
the rest of my days
without buoyancy or grace

## Things That Suddenly Matter

An unfinished scrabble board abandoned on the kitchen
     table.
A plate of egg and toast in the sink, untouched.
A cat lounging in the laundry basket.
A dog yapping in the yellow field.
A swimming pool, it's blueness an unmistakable hue of
     blue.
Two boys swimming, snorting, screaming.
Shower mist on the bathroom mirror, obscuring the face
     of the drowning day.
Faint scent of shaving cream.
A vintage Noxzema jar, cobalt, for sale on eBay.

Six winged seraphim soaring above a houseboat in
     Srinagar.
Roti made with ghee.
Homeless children sleeping in the streets.
A coconut shell filled with copper coins.
My tongue dry like a housefly in a light summer frock.
Tweezers, shears, scissors, razors, blades, scalpels.
Ashes, scattered.
The letter Y mislaid, forlorn.

*five*

What we feel primarily is our inability to feel adequately.
—Abraham Heschel

## Stress Positions

*The sword without and terror within.*
                        —*Deuteronomy 32:25*

In yoga, when limbs tremble and bend,
I rest in child's pose and dwell on stress
positions pressed on prisoners. My slight
discomfort weighed against their agony.

In tree pose, I'm a tent post in a muddy
bivouac. I confine my limbs in eagle pose,
as limbless orphans concoct makeshift sports.
In crow pose, I see flocks of stateless refugees

who occupy camps where small caged birds
are the preferred pets. Lying in corpse pose
I wonder how many graves are lost at sea.
My sorrow useless as a prayer.

## Three-Part Breath

After a cleansing round
of Dirga Pranayama—the three-part

breath—our yoga teacher says,
*Pause and trust. There will always be*

*another inhalation.* I try
to meditate on emptiness,

receive the next lungful, ignore
my prattling mind. But instead

I brood over an ailing friend
who gasps for every breath,

gathers morphine and valium
to claim his deliverance

from respiration. He pauses only
long enough to square his affairs.

In the studio's stillness,
I hear his whisper,

*Breathing is the last thing*
*you forget to do.*

## Fifty Breaths

Sit.

*breathe in, breathe out*

An empty mind is a pleasant companion.
No thought, no struggle.
Spring water to parched throat.

*breathe in, breathe out*

If you cannot not think, observe.
Thin white slats of window blinds, slightly ajar, how many?
Count bolted screws holding whirling fan to ceiling.

*breathe in, breathe out*

Remember the job you once had sewing zippers into
    jackets
in a factory where the boss locked you in at lunchtime.
Don't think of the Triangle Shirtwaist Factory.

*breathe in, breathe out*

Your son, alive and well with children of his own.
He doesn't need you now.
Nothing needs you. Rejoice.

*breathe in, breathe out*

Slide gently back to this moment.
Be as empty as a starved starling.
Balance on the edge of an avalanche.

*breathe in, breathe out*

Think thoughts neither high nor low.
Awaken to how desire destroys each present moment.
Close your eyes and see the Stygian negative of light.

*breathe in, breathe out*

Thing Jung, think shadow side, stop thinking, be shadow.
You won't escape suffering.
Don't try. Just be here. Now.

*breathe in, breathe out*

Observe rain droplets easing down the glass,
glistening like slug trails, and beyond, grey strips of sky,
boughs of fir bending as in prayer.

*breathe in, breathe out*

Think of the workers who make the shirts
and slats, as they sit at their stations, repeating
gestures in grueling 12-hour shifts.

*breathe in, breathe out*

Be repentant.
Be exultant.
Be nobody.

*breathe in, breathe out*

Try to be grateful for 33 breaths.
Try to be a C student.
No one said this would get easier.

*breathe in, breathe out*

There are six breaths left.
Resist shifting on the cushion.
Wiggle your toes to wake them.

*breathe in*

Experience attachment and let it go three times.
Experience craving and let it go three times.
Experience suffering and let it go three times.

*breathe out*

Experience bliss.
Let it go.
Three times.

## "My Body's in Trouble" *

I was in the kitchen chopping onions
when Jeff Buckley's cover of Hallelujah
burst from the radio and landed
a powerful blow to my sternum.

I lived in the East Village when Jeff
was playing the clubs down there
but I was busy watching a generation
die of AIDS and never caught his act.

Can you say which is worse: Jeff's
drowning, your best friend dying of AIDS,
or your girlfriend dumping you for some
bimbo two days after the funeral?

I wish someone would wrench
*a broken hallelujah* from my lips,
but where does it all lead except
more deaths, more to lose?

*You don't know what love is* rose up in my throat
as my knife sliced, making me feel like a hollow
bullet. But when I heard Jeff's voice, I raised
my arms high like church and began to howl.

I couldn't stop sobbing
though my eyes stung like wasps
and my head felt stuffed with bees.
And you know how I hate to cry.

*Lyrics: Mary Margaret O'Hara, Leonard Cohen,
Billie Holiday*

# Are You Ready?

*Prepare yourself for an ordeal.*
                            *—Ecclesiasticus 2*

Expect your brother's friend to rape you
in the basement. Prepare for your father to split
without farewell. Know that your mother
will die at the worst possible moment

or if she lives long, you will cause
her enormous grief. Expect to run
out of gas on the night highway, with only
thieves on a deserted road where

you will lose your soul along with
your shoes, your traveling companion,
and your name, and without a name,
you cannot board the plane. Train

for comedy and calamity, but beware
of comfort, it conspires to make us
foolish and to do foolish things like fall
in love and have children. Prepare

for the ordeal of living, with its shelling
news of wars and famine, a genocide
or two each decade, and closer to home,
betrayal by one who said she loved you.

# In Praise of That Which Doesn't Kill
*—for the Rohingya*

Thinking about all the gay men who committed
suicide because of the times, the conspiracies
of silence, the shame of not belonging
in the crowded nests of family, the group photo
of beaming bathers at the shore, the straight
poets who won all the prizes. If time had her way,
I would not be worrying today why I don't belong
in this world. And then, to make matters worse,
I learn that Buddhists can be terrorists too,
monks with guns under saffron robes,
killing and exiling their particular others.

# *six*

Because it is bitter,
And because it is my heart.
—Stephen Crane

# DNA

Coupling ensnares life, a thing being no thing
lacking contact with other things. Once paired, now
    parted,
a single-stranded lover pleads *where did you go?*

Each genome is spliced with delicate knitting. In this,
the origami heron outflies the soaring hawk. This helix
called love. A very different thing than I once imagined.

## Anhedonia

I have no talent for pleasure.
My skin rebuffs touch. Plunking
through weeks of days, the music
goes *bleep, bleep, bleep*. Even the sea
has lost its brine. Ticking off senses
one by one as they wither. Spring returns,
the forsythia fail to astonish.

I once loved long morning drives
along winding country roads,
as the sun swelled centimeter
by centimeter through seasons,
until for one week, a blinding blaze,
and then its pale retreat. Wondering
what happens to fields of corn stalks
turned under, leaves that drain green
to reveal bursts of orange, delight
at winter's first snow.

When I was still trying
to undress the universe
and know her.

# Famous

my secret is famous now, it was no mistake, I was born of it,
dragged out with forceps, the difficult one who bites,
dour pickle-faced receiver of third-place ribbons
and hand-me-downs,
solemn child from continents of changing borders
and endless wars, a legend like my eyes,
green flecked with small twigs,
a forest of hair sprouting in flocks,
that first bloody enigma, a slapped face,
a warning in Yiddish,
the shaft-of-light halo barely enough to read in bed,
eyes that never adjusted to full darkness or radiant light,
never saw constellations of the Southern sky,
stars that trailed Moses
with the unruliness of wiry hair, lice-shaven head, disgrace,
deceit, it's all there in the rumors, the night terrors,
scrubbing the rug I vomited on when home alone
with pneumonia,
*A Child's Garden of Verse*, my only expiation,
exactly how far back does a secret grow famous
without its co-conspirators,
the stillbirths that preceded me, the child with clotted
tongue, horse-lipped,
puree pouring from nostrils, the blazing house afire,
the *hush-hush* cancers, rationing oleo,
loss of faith, maiden aunts housed in refugee camps
for the insane, gamblers and infidels, how I've learned to
embellish, to make famous,
what you never told me

# Street

Maybe your mother didn't want another girl or they
tracked you beneath your abilities in fourth grade, maybe
you were dyslexic or just bored and skipped school
and got caught shoplifting, maybe you once wanted to
be a dancer, a porn star, a drummer in a girl band, but
instead became a waitress or had an abortion or a baby
when you were sixteen, or maybe you were plenty smart
but focused on solving problems of the soul and never
got very far, never connected, always felt the Jew or the
lesbian, the weirdo, maybe you always had bad luck
in love or your best friends have all died of overdoses
or AIDS, or maybe you started reading poetry too late
after too many novels and too much therapy, maybe you
couldn't share in ordinary enthusiasm for pop stars or
football, couldn't keep a job, couldn't enjoy sex, couldn't
hold your liquor, couldn't pray, couldn't believe things
would get better, did not find the key, gave away the key,
lost the key, have lost the key so many times, maybe you
learned to live without a door.

## True Story

A toothache had me by the throat,
rammed my head against the wall, flung me
to the ground, crushed my skull … and so forth.

I was 20 and broke. I went to the free clinic.
*Said, please take this damn tooth out of my mouth.*
*And he said, first you give me a blow job.*

With that mouth. And I did.

# Eviction Hearing

I had to split that juke joint.
In the crapper: odor of gonorrhea,
after-clap of stale beer and tobacco.

Down the street, a woman, cell at left ear,
mouth a-flap. Nearby, bottle-blue buzzing.
Is this an effect of the exceptionally clear
fall day or an accumulation of cerumen?

At the eviction hearing the landlord sputters,
*and leave the damn place broom-clean!*
Pushed aside with detritus, swept
into a pile of dusty gloom on linoleum.

In exchange for the bed, I let him fuck me.
Then, daylight again, I script a blueprint
of the neighborhood in one dimension—
flatlands drawn in vein-blue lies.

I visit the doctor who decrees,
*There's nothing wrong with you,*
*swallow these pills, think voodoo,*
then snaps manila wings shut and exits,
exam door left.

## Raspberry Jam

It's maraschino red,
so red you can't help but think
it's insincere. Reminds me of ketchup
in Copenhagen, perfect foil for those Danish
sausages that astonish with chubby flavor.
Or the blood of afterbirth. This jam, in its tiny rectangle,
reminds me of the Sunflour Cafe in Seattle
and the enormous affection I reserve for breakfast.
And tragically, it reminds me of you in Miami,
wet from shower in ruby robe.

## Preceded by Decades of Distance,
## Love Trounced

Last night, broken a bit by sentiment
(*which Lord knows I loathe*) we had barely
embraced, when I blurted out: *No. Don't touch me.*
You were gentle, but deep in my past, I plunged
my face into a fist, was frozen by a hostile kiss,
and for years, rebuffed all touch. But here, the miracle
of being seen while longing to be seen! The wash
of attentiveness, that careful stitch of moments
disposed to skim past each other. But flattened,
the way a photo exposes the stillness
of flowing lava and tectonic plates
hold tight in their tentative permanence.

You are to me a gem that has wrought
great damage in its excavation.

## About the Body and What It Needs

I navigate by shadows of clouds in the ocean.
I don't need a mother or lover to enter my vessel,
or to amend legends that were never mine.

I don't recall labor pains, but still feel the rush
of milk tumble into empty breasts—a small shiver
of memory that sates longing, leaves me engorged.

You must wonder how I say these things that seem
so faded. In full sight of your fraught wish to be loved
in body, my rebuff must affront you.

I will not be coy—I know it does. Since,
if these things about me were not true,
I could shower sticky kisses all over you.

I am no more alone than Emily Dickinson.
There is no idiom for the seasonal way I sail
into myself. The clouds are blue today.

## Discalced

I scour the hours you've renounced, trace
the faint trajectory of your absence, ache
for the loneliness of our intimacy—

the ruptured husk of us. I pull the single
boot you've left behind onto the wrong
foot, limping room to room.

This odd caesura of snow, dampening
sounds and scents, milky baby's breath,
crisp white noise inside icy stillness.

# seven

Whenever it will be it will be now
its own now
—C. K. Williams

## Faith in Clouds

Because they are cotton puffs
that don't support the weight of angels

Because they are shifty
and can't be trusted to warn us of heavenly squalls

Because there is a vista beyond them
called universe

Because aircraft can fly right through them
and not vanish

Because they can hold the rain, but know
when to let go

## Morning Songs

Morning rose too soon
crooned *get-up, get-up, get-up*—
heed the warbler's trill.

~~~

Morning sky suffused with rain
dripping its grey load into the choppy bay.
Mountain-clouds, muddled morning thoughts,
stiff limbs, coffee cup. Will I make it
through the tumble of this day, through
these somersaults of days?

~~~

Morning is broken
like cracked eggs
spilt milk on the countertop
library books gone missing
silk blouse stained with black ink
muddled dreams vanished
keys left in the door
from the night before.

~~~

This bluet Monday morning
I flirted with you and wore a dress
(something I never do).

You saw right through me
(pillars of brains and breasts)
and knew I wasn't wearing

underwear. You hugged me
snug against your chest,
an invisible floret between us,
forever deflowered.

## Bread

I'm not hungry
but I want bread,
the crust and batting of bread
in my mouth, silk of butter
on my tongue.

I don't need the body,
just the spirit, to fill this hollow
made of teeth
with the manna of its ever-
readiness to console.

# Faith Healing at the MB Caschetta
# Writers Group Retreat

We scribble in desperation, words trickle or gush from cut
jugulars. We write to heal, but writing doesn't cure, it
    congeals.
We drown and breach to retrieve our own sacred essence.

Alone, each treads the stations of her private cross. We
fear everything known, and then, the unknowable. Failure,
rejection, success. We don't know what will be said
    about us, and so

we fear gossip, derision, unkind reviews. We eat meals
together, sisters confessing our slightest sins, hoping
to be forgiven. We admit we have too often failed
    to forgive.

In the evenings, we share the words we have managed
to wring from tapped-out psyches during daylight. The
night welcomes us to rest, we lie on couches, drink tea.

On our last night, without a script, we enter a state
of grace and perform faith healings for one another.
We lay on hands, pray, offer blessings.

The road home looms ahead as daunting as the road
we took to get here. There is still much to dread.

## Shocked
*—for Thomas Merton*

I see his bare chest, fresh from shower,
towel wrapped and tucked at waist, glancing
around the cloistered room, the single cot,
the modest writing desk, the tall fan—

then quietly reaching to turn it on, rotate
the wings of prayer, spinning west to east
last thoughts perhaps of wind storms and aridity—
and that current buzzing through his body

staying the precious heart, that monk of a man
who bore on his broad Trappist shoulders the yoke
of Jesus and Buddha embracing—it must have been
a mouth-watering surprise.

## On Leaving the Barn Door Open

In 1994, when Leonard Cohen danced me to the end
then split
and holed up for six years
on Mount Baldy, afraid of losing nothing,
which he never found,

I missed him as sorely as I missed my son,
kidnapped from my arms, the women who've left me
loveless,
J's amethyst ring lost on a Greyhound bus.

I've compressed my losses
by leaning on imagery and verse,
by my own version of hermitude,
by renouncing ordinary eros.

It's the slight headache, the worry
I've lived the wrong life, the fear
of not being able to fill my days with thoughts
the fear of not being able to stop thoughts
the thought itself, like a scalpel

carving into white matter saying,
*This here is an irreversible mistake.*
*There will be no do-overs.*

Will I limp through two more
decades with no conjugation
of any sort?

# Jezebel

I've not replaced Jezebel,
who died in my arms
with a needle in her paw

years ago. On this dismal
wintry day, shag of snow
in the yard, I'm on my own.

As my last lover shut
the door, she warned,
*You'll die pet-less and unwed.*

Now I live like a nun
who's slept too many nights
in a habit of coarse cloth.

## Again, I Climb

Again, I climb
the crest of the last rise
before the road twists its way
downhill to the bay.

She lifts into view, her frosted top floating,
as these Pacific Northwest peaks will do,
a mirage above a shimmering cake stand,
and without blush I confess to her—
*O my dear, dear Mount Baker.*

I also fling blessings at the moon
when it delights me, emerging full
from behind a cloud in leaden sky
to guide me home again.

The me that only sings or cries
alone in the car foresees the day I will not
round this curve again, not drive again,
not see mountaintops again, have to leave
my home for the sheltered hovels of the old,
fated to never see the moon again and again,
and then, to not see again.

# Rain

Most days, I no longer long
for you. The rain has become
my welcome mat.

I soak clothes and skin in it,
bleach these personal stains, staunch
my body's needs.

I dream in haiku
as it taps at my window
in tart syllables.

Nowhere is it fully
documented how terrifying it is
to be me.

## When I'm not thinking about you,
## I learn the names of trees

I've learned to tell the fir from the yew; the silver
from the red cedar. At sunrise, there is a thin glint of light
northeastward where I await Mt Baker's frozen specter

careening over Discovery Bay. The lamps of Port
Townsend blink; strands of fog hang over fields.
Peckish deer nibble dandelions. I spare my lawn

for their graze. The squirrels, miniature and rust-bellied,
easily reach the hanging bird seed. I don't try to learn
bird calls, they come to feed and that's enough.

There are rumors of big cats. I've seen two elk—
one stared through me as if she knew my secrets, the other,
roadkill. You once told me my poems are too grim

and I should try my hand at something more pastoral.
I've seen powdered snow on Cedars, and I've grown
passably fond of rain. Everyday, the clouds amaze.

## Tisha b'Av

these are days of awe, we fast and mourn, fast and atone
my bed is north, my love is south
I break my fast with broth

I sip tea and wait for the waitress to serve the bland soup
the curve of a coke bottle arouses pleasure
a brown sweetness, a time for everything

cane sugar, cocaine, crack, sea-green glass
my bed is empty, my love flies east
I cannot eat the soup for the slipperiness of hope

risk skims its needle smoothly into a vein
I am the eye, the pistil, the sadness
the store-bought flowers in their paper wrap

snow rimes my bed, my love slowly chills
a waning crescent hangs low in the west
here, here is my list of sins

# Notes

In "Metanoia Lost" metanoia refers to a spiritual conversion such as the conversion of Paul on the road to Damascus.

"Charoset and Bitter Herbs" and horseradish are three of the symbolic foods eaten at the Passover Seder.

"Yellow Star" references the 1911 fire at the Triangle Shirtwaist Factory in New York City.

"Tisha b'Av" is a fast day on the Jewish Calendar, commemorating the destruction of the first and second Temples in Jerusalem.

# Acknowledgments

The author wishes to thank the following online and print journals and publishers who have previously published original versions of these poems, some in earlier versions or with different titles.

*13 Myna Birds:* "Map of Death by Drowning"

*Academy of American Poets:* "Ice Would Suffice"

*Agape Editions:* "How to Be Sad"

*American Journal of Nursing:* "Three-Part Breath"

*Arsenic Lobster:* "Raspberry Jam"

*Autumn Sky Review:* "Abiding Winter;" "Again, I Climb;" "'Body of Well-Known Naturalist Found in River'"

*Blue Lyra Review:* "Tisha b'Av"

*Calyx:* "Street"

*Cascadia Review:* "Mean Distance from the Sun, Mid-Winter, Northern Hemisphere"

*Contemporary American Voices:* "Saving Moses"

*Escape into Life:* "Discalced;" "Shocked"

*HIV Here & Now World AIDS Day 2017:* "The Night We Tossed Your Ashes"

*In My Exam Room* (The Lives You Touch Publications)*:* "'Even the Gorgeous Royal Chariots Wear Out';" "When I'm not thinking of you, I learn the names of trees"

*Ithaca Lit Review:* "DNA;" "Mourning After Murders;" "Nostalgia is an illness you might die of;" "Swimming Lesson"

*Jewish Currents:* "Famous"

*Lavender Review:* "About the Body and What It Needs;" "Before World;" "Faith Healing at the MB Caschetta Writers Group Retreat;" "On Leaving the Barn Door Open;" "Yellow Star"

*LiTFUSE Anthology:* "Formation"

*Leaf Press:* "Life Forms Evolving"

*Mean Distance from the Sun* (Aldrich Press): "Camels and Iced Coffee;" "Rain"

*Menacing Hedge:* "Bimbo, deer"

*One:* "Tracings"

*Pittsburgh Poetry Review:* "Quarter-Mile Church"

*Raven Chronicles:* "In Search of Home"

*Silver Birch Press:* "Outsider"

*SoundZine:* "Anhedonia"

*Spry:* "Twenty Years of Dead"

*The New Verse News:* "Diaspora"

*The Longleaf Pine:* "Southern Faith"

*The Nervous Breakdown:* "Metanoia Lost"

*The Rumpus:* "How Two Trees Become a Forest"

*Whirlwind @ Lesbos* (Headmistress Press): "To a woman I might have loved"

## About the Author

Risa Denenberg was born in Washington DC in 1950 and has lived in Miami & Tallahassee Florida, New York City, and rural Pennsylvania prior to moving to the Pacific Northwest in 2008. She is a nurse practitioner who has worked for more than four decades in diverse health care settings including women's health, HIV/AIDS, chronic pain, and hospice and palliative care. She volunteers with End of Life Washington, the advocacy group that supports Washington state's Death with Dignity Law.

Denenberg reviews poems for the *American Journal of Nursing* and is a cofounder and editor at Headmistress Press, an independent publisher of books of poetry by lesbians. She is the author of three chapbooks and two prior full-length poetry collections, *Mean Distance from the Sun* (Aldrich Press, 2014) and *Whirlwind @ Lesbos* (Headmistress Press, 2016).

She currently lives with her cat, Bo, in a place of stunning beauty on the Olympic peninsula. From her writing desk, she looks out at Discovery Bay and, on a clear day, she can see Mount Baker in the distance. She enjoys yoga, cooking, drawing, and reading.

Follow Risa's blog at risaden.wordpress.com.

CPSIA information can be obtained
at www.ICGtesting.com
Printed in the USA
BVHW04s1148070518
515500BV00005B/662/P

9 781936 657353